Cello Time Sprinters

a third book of pieces for cello

Kathy and David Blackwell

Grateful thanks are due to Alison Ingram and Tom Morter
for all their help with this volume.

Welcome to **Cello Time Sprinters**. You'll find:

- extended pieces in first position
- fourth position pieces using the finger patterns 1–34, 12–4, and 1234
- a range of techniques, e.g. hooked bowing, string crossing, and double-stops
- original pieces in different styles plus pieces by a range of composers
- duets with parts of equal difficulty
- scales and arpeggios to suit the pieces and at the level of Grade 3
- Performances and backings for all the pieces, many with drumkit and bass added, as well as tuning tracks, available to download from a Companion Website: www.oup.com/ctsprinters
- straightforward piano accompaniments available in a separate volume

Pieces with piano accompaniment are presented in two formats on the Companion Website: firstly, a complete performance, then the accompaniment only, which you can play along to. There is a count-in when the cello and piano parts start together.

This symbol is placed alongside all the pieces for which audio tracks are available to download from the Companion Website. For all duets, there is a track with the top part only and a track with the lower part only, so that you can play along with either part.

This symbol indicates which pieces have a piano accompaniment (published in a separate volume).

MUSIC DEPARTMENT

OXFORD
UNIVERSITY PRESS

OXFORD
UNIVERSITY PRESS

Great Clarendon Street, Oxford OX2 6DP, England
198 Madison Avenue, New York, NY10016, USA

Oxford University Press is a department of the University of Oxford.
It furthers the University's aim of excellence in research, scholarship,
and education by publishing worldwide

Oxford is a registered trade mark of Oxford University Press
in the UK and in certain other countries

© Oxford University Press 2005

Kathy and David Blackwell have asserted their right under the Copyright, Designs
and Patents Act, 1988, to be identified as the Composers of this Work.

Database right Oxford University Press (maker)

First published 2005

All rights reserved. No part of this publication may be reproduced,
stored in a retrieval system, or transmitted, in any form or by any means,
without the prior permission in writing of Oxford University Press,
or as expressly permitted by law. Enquiries concerning reproduction
outside the scope of the above should be sent to the Music Copyright
Department, Oxford University Press, at the address above

Permission to perform the works in this anthology in public
(except in the course of divine worship) should normally be obtained
from the Performing Right Society Ltd. (PRS), 29/33 Berners Street,
London W1T 3AB, or its affiliated Societies in each country throughout
the world, unless the owner or the occupier of the premises
being used holds a licence from the Society

Permission to make a recording must be obtained in advance
from the Mechanical-Copyright Protection Society Ltd. (MCPS),
Elgar House, 41 Streatham High Road, London SW16 1ER,
or its affiliated Societies in each country throughout the world

20

ISBN 0–19–322115–2

Music and text origination by
Barnes Music Engraving Ltd., East Sussex

Printed in Great Britain on acid-free paper by
Halstan & Co. Ltd., Amersham, Bucks.

All pieces are original compositions by the authors unless stated otherwise.

Contents

First position
1. Carnival jig 4
2. Spic and span 4
3. Out of the question (*duet*) 5
4. Stop—start 6
5. River song 6
6. Overture: A Baroque celebration 7

Fourth position: 1–34
7. Going fourth 8
8. City streets 8
9. Minuet (Mozart) (*duet*) 9
10. Metro line 10
11. Falling leaves 10
12. Holiday in Havana 11
13. Swing low, sweet chariot (*duet*) 12
14. Night shift 13
15. Le Tambourin (Rameau) 13
16. Scarborough Fair (*duet*) 14
17. Beyond the horizon 15
18. Sto me 15

Fourth position: 12–4
19. Bourrée (Stölzel) (*duet*) 16
20. Andante (Elgar) 17
21. Joker in the pack 17
22. Sarabande (Handel) (*duet*) 18
23. Comin' home 19
24. Sprint finish 20
25. In memory 20

Fourth position: 1234
26. Some day 21
27. Wild West 22
28. Je pense à toi 23
29. Russian wedding 24
30. Two Songs from Dichterliebe (Schumann) 25
31. Latin nights 26
32. 4th dimension 27
33. Fifth Avenue 28

Study and rounds
34. Seventh heaven 29
35. Jubilate Deo (Mozart) 29
36. Banuwa 29

Scales and Arpeggios 30

1. Carnival jig

2. Spic and span

Variation: try playing with 2 semiquavers to each note:

3. Out of the question

Play questions and answers in this duet, returning to the chorus after each verse.
Make up and write down a question and answer of your own in the 3rd verse. Add your own dynamics!

4. Stop—start

5. River song

6. Overture

A Baroque celebration

7. Going fourth

KB & DB

Andante

2 — 0 — *mf* — 1 — *p*

7 — 0 — *mf* — 1 — *p*

11 — 0 — *mf* — 1 — *p* — **rit.**

8. City streets

KB & DB

Driving

3 — *mf* (*p*)

7 — 1 — *cresc.*

12 — *f* — 0

16 — *mf* — **poco rall.** — 1 — *mp dim.* — *pp*

9. Minuet

Allegretto

W. A. Mozart (1756–91)

10. Metro line

11. Falling leaves

12. Holiday in Havana

Warm up

Play a G major scale in the rumba rhythm:

13. Swing low, sweet chariot

Spiritual

Play the second chorus as a canon, with the second part entering after a minim at *.
Count carefully in bar 20! Also try as a canon in 3 or 4 parts.

14. Night shift

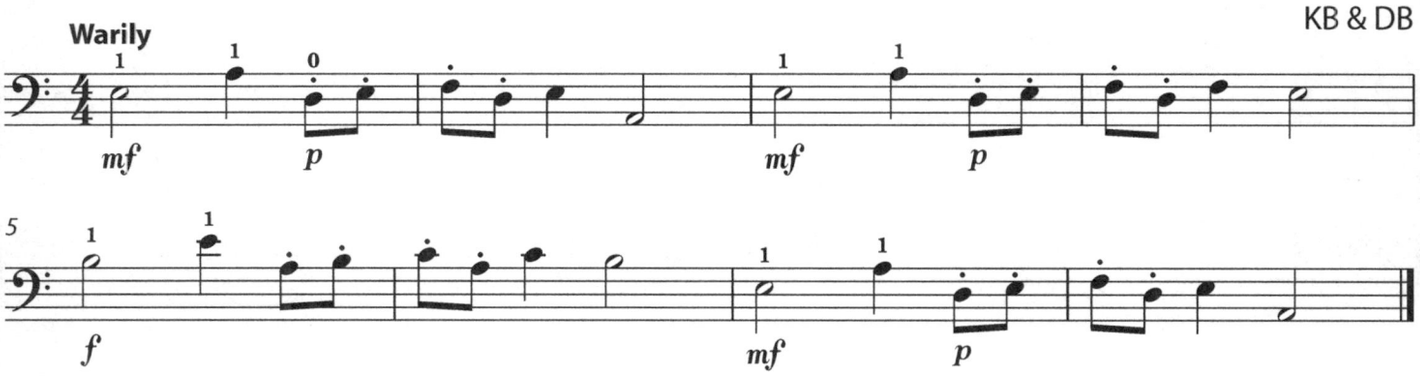

15. Le Tambourin

A tambourin was a lively 18th-century French dance, often accompanied by pipe and tabor.

16. Scarborough Fair

English trad.

17. Beyond the horizon

18. Sto me

A backing track for a version of the piece transposed up a fifth to A minor is available on the Companion Website. Try playing it by ear—here's the start:

19. Bourrée

G. H. Stölzel (1690–1749)

Adapted from the Clavierbüchlein for Wilhelm Friedemann Bach.

20. Andante

Edward Elgar (1857–1934)

21. Joker in the pack

KB & DB

22. Sarabande

G. F. Handel (1685–1759)
(adapted)

23. Comin' home

24. Sprint finish

25. In memory

(*for Eileen*)

26. Some day

27. Wild West

Warm up

Sort out the F naturals and F sharps, and B naturals and B flats in this piece before you start.

28. Je pense à toi

(for Clare)

Think of the timbre and dynamic changes as you play the repeat phrase in 1st and 4th position.

29. Russian wedding

30. Two Songs from Dichterliebe

1. The lovely month of May

Robert Schumann (1810–56)
(adapted)

2. The rose and the lily

31. Latin nights

Tango

KB & DB

32. 4th dimension

KB & DB

Warm up

Play an F major scale in the rhythm of the opening bar—don't play on the first beat, and watch the accents!

33. Fifth Avenue

(*for Iain*)

Swing ♫ = ♪♪

KB & DB

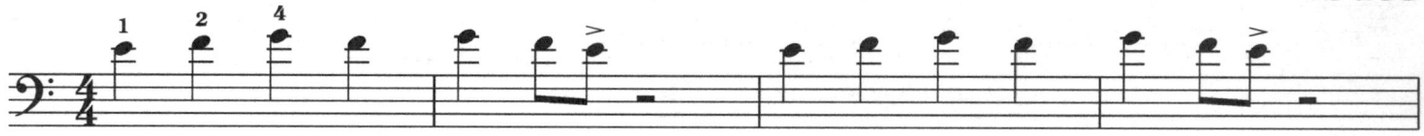

34. Seventh heaven

KB & DB

Dominant seventh study

× Tap your cello with your left hand.

35. Jubilate Deo

Play this round in 2 or more parts, entering at *:

W. A. Mozart (1756–91)

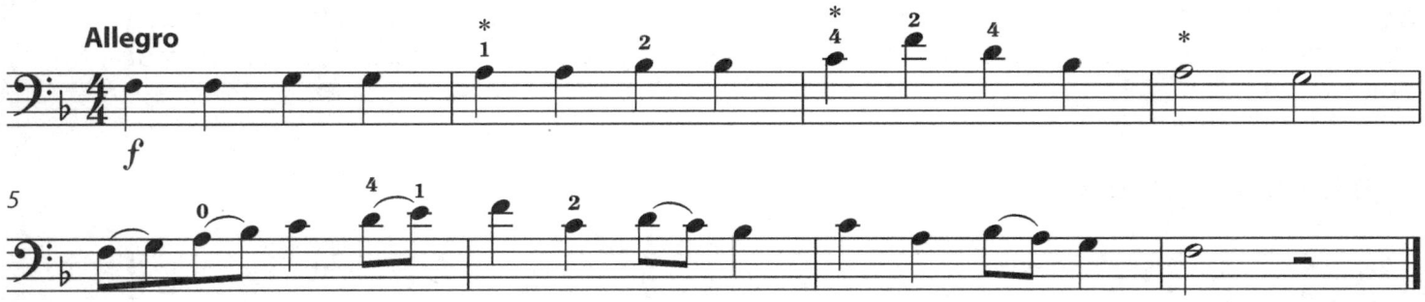

36. Banuwa

Play this round in 2 or more parts, entering at *:

African

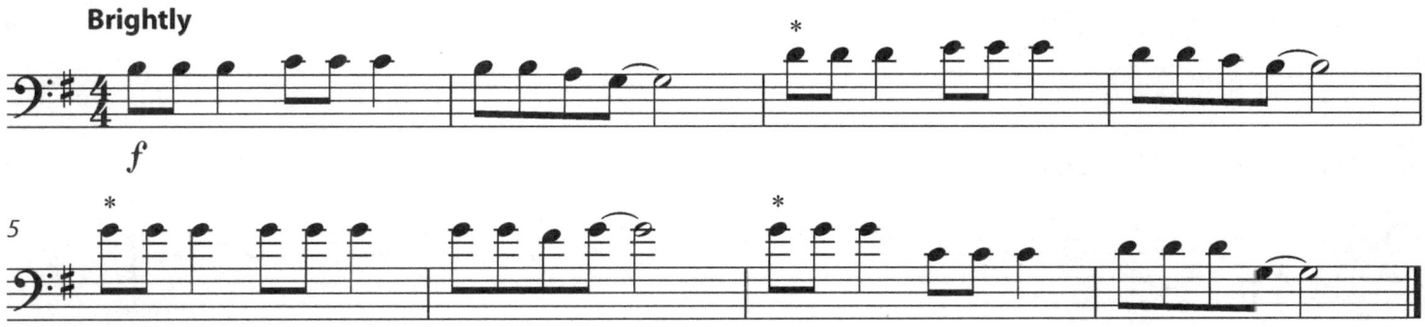

Scales and Arpeggios

A major scale 1 octave

A major arpeggio 1 octave

B♭ major scale 1 octave

B♭ major arpeggio 1 octave

C harmonic minor scale 1 octave

C melodic minor scale 1 octave

C minor arpeggio 1 octave

G harmonic minor scale 1 octave

G melodic minor scale 1 octave

G minor arpeggio 1 octave

D major scale 2 octaves

D major arpeggio 2 octaves

C major scale 2 octaves

C major arpeggio 2 octaves

D harmonic minor scale 2 octaves

D melodic minor scale 2 octaves

D minor arpeggio 2 octaves

G major scale 2 octaves

G major arpeggio 2 octaves

F major scale 2 octaves

F major arpeggio 2 octaves

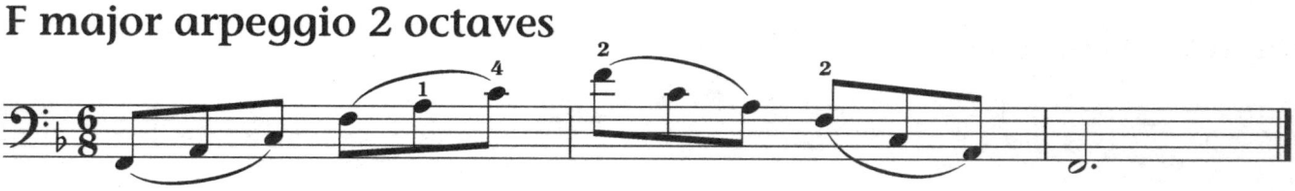

Dominant 7th in the key of F

Dominant 7th in the key of C

Dominant 7th in the key of G